MW01247400

RED
LETTER
CHURCH

DOING
CHURCH
THE
JESUS
WAY

RED
LETTER
CHURCH.
ORG

All Bible references are from the World English Bible

Printed in the United States of America

First Printing, 2023

ISBN 979-8-218-35053-6

Wriote Publishing
9990 Coconut Rd.
Bonita Springs, FL 34135

support@redletterchurch.org

DOWNLOAD A FREE COPY OF THIS BOOK

If you go to **RedLetterChurch.org** you can download a free copy of this book. If you want a hard copy of this book then it can be purchased on **Amazon.com**.

TABLE OF CONTENTS

INTRODUCTION

WHAT IS A RED LETTER CHURCH?

The Conversation

Jesus has been provoking me to write this book for over 20 years. I don't feel worthy to write about these topics, so I have neglected doing so. However, a recent conversation with my oldest son prompted me to finally put the proverbial pen to paper. My son, who is now 14, has seen how we do church his entire life (we started our church before he was born), and he wanted to know where we fit in the broader context of Christianity. He asked me which denomination we share the most in common with.

It was a difficult question to answer.

I told him the many things that I respect about Catholics, Protestants, and other expressions of Christianity, but I couldn't in good faith tell him that what we were doing could easily be compared to the most popular versions of Christianity that he is likely to encounter. He probed, as 14 year olds do. He wanted to know the essential differences between other denominations and what he had seen first hand his entire life.

Wanting to give an honest and clear answer to a young man who is seeking the truth, I told him that we envision church through the words of Jesus, where other denominations use Jesus as only one of their sources, and many times, not the primary source.

He wanted examples.

We talked for hours that night as we explored a Jesus centered gospel, Jesus centered mission, Jesus centered discipleship, and Jesus centered community. I ultimately told him that we are a part of a Red Letter Church (RLC), a phrase I had never used before.

The verse that I kept referring to was in John 15:14 where Jesus does something that we often overlook. He equated a love for him with an obedience to his commands. We are so quick to view love as an emotion, and obedience as legalism, that we have a hard time even reading this command of Jesus and taking it seriously.

> **John 15:14**
>
> *If you love me, keep my commandments.*

My son asked why I didn't try to popularize my views, and he noted how there was something different about what we are doing, and that the world needs to hear about it. I quickly responded by listing the many people that I had personally taught, mentored, baptized, and trained, but he wasn't satisfied. He challenged me to write something that would give even more people a chance to be a part of a Red Letter Church.

This book is the product of that conversation. Whether you are thinking of starting a new church, reforming an existing church, or simply trying to understand what Christianity is all about, I hope this book challenges you to consider everything through the lens of Jesus.

The Framework

This book is divided into four sections, each corresponding to a different function of the church that should be reimagined through the words of Jesus: **Gospel**, **Mission**, **Discipleship**, and **Community**. Below is a visual that might be helpful:

The cross serves as a visual for the four things the church does, and the four natural directions of those things.

- **Gospel**: The church looks up, to preach the gospel of the kingdom like Jesus.
- **Mission**: The church looks forward, into the future, to make new disciples like Jesus.
- **Discipleship**: The church looks down, inward, to be people who live like Jesus.
- **Community**: The church looks back, to the community that is already committed, to gather like Jesus.

The premise of this book may seem tame, but If you take the ideas seriously that you are about to encounter then you will find yourself in an authentic expression of church that is radically different than anything you have experienced before. Red Letter Churches don't require the trappings found in most Western churches:

- Red Letter Churches don't require a budget.
- Red Letter Churches don't require a building.
- Red Letter Churches don't require a band.
- Red Letter Churches don't require a theological degree.
- Red Letter Churches don't require a professional speaker.

- Red Letter Churches don't require a logo and a website.

- Red Letter Churches don't require founding documents and statements of beliefs.

- Red Letter Churches don't require a legal entity to be formed, like an LLC or a 501(c)3.

These may seem like fringe niceties, but they are far from it. From the immense simplicity and depth of Red Letter Churches comes a potential for growth that is unparalleled in the Christian world. Complicated things don't spontaneously replicate. There is a reason the early church went from about 25,000 Christians in 100 AD to about 20,000,000 Christians by 300 AD. The early church was all about Jesus, not professionally planned weekly sermons and concerts. Simple things, when coupled with depth, can scale.

Whether you are offended or intrigued, I implore you to read on. The church needs you, specifically you, to get this.

In Him—Your Brother
December, 2023

P.S. If you are a part of a Red Letter Church and you want to add your church to the directory on RedLetterChurch.org then email support@redletterchurch.org.

CHAPTER 1 / GOSPEL

HOW DID JESUS DEFINE THE GOOD NEWS?

This Is Not A Trick Question

If I asked you how Jesus defined the gospel could you give me a clear and coherent answer? This isn't a "gotcha" question. He defined the gospel (also called the good news) multiple times throughout his ministry. If you answered with a version of "he died for our sins" then you would be referring to one aspect of the gospel, but it wouldn't be the primary way that Jesus defined the gospel during his ministry.

Before you decide that I am a heretic—yes, Jesus died for our sins. His death, burial, and resurrection are inseparable from the gospel. But back to the original question: If I asked you how Jesus defined the gospel could you give me a clear and coherent answer?

I'll spend the rest of this chapter defining the gospel using Jesus' own words, but first, let's consider why most Christians can't answer this simple question. We struggle with this question because churches have habitually defined the gospel in such a narrow way that it has become the punchline to a joke that we forgot to tell. Yes, the punchline is a part of a joke, but it doesn't encapsulate the entire joke.

Here's an example: If I say "Because he was outstanding in his field." Then you probably won't laugh. However, if I say, "Why did the scarecrow win the Nobel prize? Because he was outstanding in his field." Then you might laugh. A punchline, without a setup, is confusing.

The church in the west has a habit of ignoring Jesus' words about the gospel (the setup), and we interpret everything through the lens of Paul (the punchline). The problem is that Paul is often reminding his readers of the punchline to a story he developed more fully in person.

If we want to be a part of a church that takes Jesus seriously then we have to come to terms with how Jesus defined the gospel. What we discover will not be mere semantics, but rather a new paradigm to view Christianity through. Learning the truth about Jesus' gospel is the beginning of a revolution.

The Son of Man

We begin our study by looking at the phrase "Son of Man." Did you know that Jesus' favorite way to refer to himself wasn't Christ, Messiah, or God's Son? Those are all true ways to refer to Jesus, but his favorite way to refer to himself was as the Son of Man. In fact, Jesus referred to himself as the Son of Man 80 times during his ministry. This begs the question...what is the Son of Man?

At first, you might be tempted to think that the phrase Son of Man is just a way to denote Jesus' incarnation, that being God he was also man. However, this isn't the only thing the phrase means, which becomes clear when we look at where it appears in the Old Testament. The Son of Man is found in Daniel, and it's a prophecy about Jesus:

Daniel 7:13-14

I saw in the night visions, and behold, there came with the clouds of the sky one like a son of man, and he came even to the ancient of days, and they brought him near before him. Dominion was given him, and glory, and a kingdom, that all the peoples, nations, and languages should serve him. His dominion is an everlasting dominion, which will not pass away, and his kingdom one that which will not be destroyed.

Notice what Daniel says about the Son of Man:

- The Son of Man would come from above (the clouds).

- The Son of Man would be presented before God (ancient of days).

- The Son of Man would have control (dominion) over all the Earth (peoples, nations, and languages).

- The Son of Man would have glory.

- The Son of Man would have a kingdom that would never end and never be destroyed.

When Jesus refers to himself as the Son of Man 80 times, it is this Son of Man that he is referring to. The Son of Man is not a title of humility to depict the lowliness of Jesus. The Son of Man title is actually one of power that shows Jesus' unique relationship to God and his lordship over all people.

You may wonder how we know for sure that Jesus was using the title of Son of Man from the book of Daniel, instead of somewhere else. Jesus makes it clear that he is using the phrase Son of Man from the book of Daniel during his discussion with the High Priest, before he was crucified:

> **Mark 14:60-62**
>
> *The high priest stood up in the middle, and asked Jesus, "Have you no answer? What is it which these testify against you?" But he stayed quiet, and answered nothing. Again the high priest asked him, "Are you the Christ, the Son of the Blessed?"*
>
> *Jesus said, "I am. You will see the Son of Man sitting at the right hand of Power, and coming with the clouds of the sky."*

This is a perfect allusion to Daniel. Whenever Jesus calls himself the Son of Man he is claiming to be the Son of Man from Daniel, which means he is claiming to be from heaven, to have an intimate relationship to God, to have control over the Earth, to be filled with glory, and to have a kingdom that will last forever.

The Kingdom Is The Gospel

You might be wondering what any of this has to do with how Jesus defined the gospel. The connection is simply this: Jesus defined the gospel as the arrival of his kingdom from Daniel. The good news is that Jesus' kingdom (the kingdom of the Son of Man) is finally on Earth. Look at how Jesus defines the good news in his own words:

Mark 1:14-15

Now after John was taken into custody, Jesus came into Galilee, preaching the Good News of God's Kingdom, and saying, "The time is fulfilled, and God's Kingdom is at hand! Repent, and believe in the Good News."

The kingdom that was prophesied in Daniel hundreds of years before Jesus is now here on Earth, and that is the good news according to Jesus. We don't have to wait any longer for the kingdom of God to be present. It's here now (Luke 9:27). Jesus defines the good news as the arrival of the kingdom each of the seven times where he defines the good news (Matthew 4:23, Matthew 9:35, Matthew 24:14, Mark 1:14-15, Luke 4:43, Luke 8:1, Luke 16:16).

Not only did Jesus preach the good news of the kingdom, but it's also what he commanded his apostles to preach when he sent them out:

Matthew 10:7

"As you go, preach, saying, 'The Kingdom of Heaven is at hand!'"

We can even see that the early church in Acts also considered the good news to be a message about the kingdom of Jesus:

Acts 8:12

But when they believed Philip preaching good news concerning God's Kingdom and the name of Jesus Christ, they were baptized, both men and women.

The Elements Of A Kingdom

Here are the two questions we now must address: what is the kingdom of God, and why does it matter?

Kingdom is simply another word for country. Think about the UK as being an abbreviation for the United Kingdom. Canada is a kingdom. Mexico is a kingdom. You get the idea. A kingdom is its own nation. Kingdom, nation, and country, are all synonyms, and they each have the following elements: their own leader, their own citizens, and their own laws.

So who is the king of God's kingdom? Jesus.

John 18:37

Pilate therefore said to him, "Are you a king then?" Jesus answered, "You say that I am a king. For this reason I have been born, and for this reason I have come into the world, that I should testify to the truth. Everyone who is of the truth listens to my voice."

Next, who are the citizens of God's kingdom? Those who do God's will.

Matthew 7:21

"Not everyone who says to me, 'Lord, Lord,' will enter into the Kingdom of Heaven, but he who does the will of my Father who is in heaven.

What are the laws of God's kingdom? Jesus' words. Here is what Jesus says about his commands at the beginning of his Sermon on the Mount.

Matthew 5:19

Therefore, whoever shall break one of these least commandments and teach others to do so, shall be called least in the Kingdom of Heaven; but whoever shall do and teach them shall be called great in the Kingdom of Heaven.

There is one aspect of every nation that we have left out though. A nation needs land, a geographical boundary to separate it from other countries. This is why the disciples asked Jesus if he was going to restore the kingdom to Israel when he was teaching about God's kingdom (Acts 1:3,6). However, to understand Jesus' kingdom you must realize that his kingdom is not of this world. During Jesus' trial, when he was being questioned by Pontius Pilate, Jesus taught us this.

> ### John 18:36
>
> *Jesus answered, "My Kingdom is not of this world. If my Kingdom were of this world, then my servants would fight, that I wouldn't be delivered to the Jews. But now my Kingdom is not from here."*

Jesus' kingdom is a spiritual kingdom, not a geographical kingdom, so it doesn't have any boundaries.

To summarize so far, Jesus' kingdom has a leader which is Jesus, it has citizens which are those who do God's will, and it has laws which are the teachings of Jesus, but it doesn't have any geographical boundaries. Jesus kingdom is an invisible kingdom that stretches across the whole Earth for those that choose to be citizens of it.

It's worth noting that "going to heaven" and "being a part of God's kingdom" are the same thing. If you are not a part of God's kingdom now you won't be a part of God's kingdom later in heaven. Jesus simply hands over the existing kingdom to the Father at the end of time. This is how Paul explains it in his letter to the Corinthians:

> **1 Corinthians 15:24**
>
> *Then the end comes, when he [Jesus] will deliver up the Kingdom to God, even the Father, when he will have abolished all rule and all authority and power.*

Going to heaven isn't some separate act from joining the kingdom. In fact, God wants the Kingdom of heaven to come to Earth, allowing us to join it, before it is handed back to the father. That's why the Lord's Prayer says the following:

> **Matthew 6:10**
>
> *Let your Kingdom come. Let your will be done on earth as it is in heaven.*

Now for the bad news. There is a coming war, and it will be every kingdom of the Earth against Jesus' kingdom. As we saw in the Corinthian verse above, Jesus will destroy every rule and authority. Whoever stays a part of their current kingdom, and doesn't repent and join Jesus' kingdom, will be fighting a war against God. Here is how Jesus describes it in another place:

Luke 14:31-33

Or what king, as he goes to encounter another king in war, will not sit down first and consider whether he is able with ten thousand to meet him who comes against him with twenty thousand? Or else, while the other is yet a great way off, he sends an envoy, and asks for conditions of peace. So therefore whoever of you who doesn't renounce all that he has, he can't be my disciple.

Reimagining The Gospel

With everything we've looked at let me tell you the gospel story from a Jesus perspective without using any complicated religious language:

In the Old Testament a kingdom for God's people was prophesied about. It would be a kingdom that no one could destroy or overtake. Jesus is the leader of this kingdom and his good news is that this kingdom is now present on Earth. It's not a geographical kingdom, but rather a spiritual kingdom. Jesus is the leader of this kingdom, his commands are the laws of this kingdom, and we are invited to be citizens of this kingdom. The citizens of God's kingdom are sometimes called disciples, Christians, or believers, but these all mean the same thing. Jesus's sacrifice on the cross forgave the sins of his kingdom citizens. It's important to be a part of God's kingdom because it will be handed over to God at the end of time. If you are not in God's kingdom now then you won't be in God's kingdom later. God's kingdom will outlast every other kingdom, and Jesus is the only ruler or authority that will be in power forever. If you stay a citizen of your current kingdom then you will be on the wrong side of the coming war.

So is the good news that Jesus died for our sins? Obviously, that's a part of the good news. The king of the everlasting kingdom died for his citizens' sins. But if you skip the good news of the kingdom, and jump straight to the punchline of the cross, then you will misread virtually everything in the New Testament.

When you read the scriptures, with the kingdom in mind, you will realize that every time the kingdom is mentioned that it's actually a verse for you, and it's a verse that pertains to your gospel and your salvation. As a test, go and read Paul's words in Galatians 5:19-21. It's hard to ignore these verses now, isn't it? I recommend you re-read the entire New Testament soon. Every single verse about the kingdom is about you and your salvation.

The call of the gospel is to change your citizenship. If you still think, as a Christian, that being an American is where your citizenship is at then you don't understand the good news of the kingdom. Our goal is not to be a part of, or reform, an existing nation, but rather to be a part of God's nation. This is why I will not pledge allegiance to any flag. My allegiance is to a different kingdom, God's kingdom.

When the church wakes up and realizes that the good news we get to be a part of is actually a subversive and counter-cultural nation that is led by Jesus, then maybe our lives will start looking a little different. The gospel is not about inviting people to church—it's about inviting people to a new nation. This is why Jesus told us to seek first his kingdom (Matt 6:33), not religion, national pride, or anything else.

Even Paul, who people sometimes assume didn't preach the gospel of the kingdom like Jesus did, is actually on record as preaching about the kingdom with boldness for two years straight. We'll come back to this point later, but Paul and Jesus taught the same gospel and their messages never contradicted. This would make sense since a disciple is not above his teacher (Luke 6:40).

Acts 28:30-31

Paul stayed two whole years in his own rented house and received all who were coming to him, preaching God's Kingdom, and teaching the things concerning the Lord Jesus Christ with all boldness, without hindrance.

The message of the kingdom is a powerful message that takes us beyond the easy believism that we are accustomed to. Are you ready to turn the world upside down by being a citizen of God's invisible kingdom and telling the world about the true king, Jesus?

Acts 17:6-7

...they dragged Jason and certain brothers before the rulers of the city, crying, "These who have turned the world upside down have come here also, whom Jason has received. These all act contrary to the decrees of Caesar, saying that there is another king, Jesus!

CHAPTER 2 / MISSION

HOW DID JESUS TELL US TO MAKE DISCIPLES?

Confused Disciple Making

When it comes to evangelism the church at large is willing to try anything to help people become Christians...except what Jesus actually commanded us to do.

- Some churches have "seeker events" where non-believers will feel comfortable in the hopes that this will lead to them becoming Christians. Jesus never spoke about seeker events.

- Some churches adopted a "sinner's prayer" ritual where they lead people through a prayer that makes them a Christian. Jesus never spoke about the sinner's prayer.

- Some churches do an "altar call" at the end of the sermon where people can go to the stage and confess their need for God. Jesus never spoke about altar calls.

- Some churches hand out "tracts" which are clever ways to communicate the world's need for Jesus in the form of a small booklet, or on coins or fake money. Jesus never spoke about tracts.

- Some churches start "outreach coffee shops" where non-believers will visit for a cup of coffee and free wi-fi, and hopefully they will read a verse on the wall, or hear a testimony during an open mic night. Jesus never spoke about outreach coffee shops.

The Jesus Method

So if Jesus didn't command us to make disciples by using seeker events, sinner's prayers, altar calls, tracts, or coffee shops, then what did he tell us to do? Here is how Jesus told us to make disciples:

Matthew 28:18-20

Jesus came to them and spoke to them, saying, "All authority has been given to me in heaven and on earth. Go and make disciples of all nations, baptizing them in the name of the Father and of the Son and of the Holy Spirit, teaching them to observe all things that I commanded you. Behold, I am with you always, even to the end of the age." **Amen.**

If we are going to build Red Letter Churches then it's important that we slow down and actually think about the red letters, the words that Jesus actually spoke. In the above verses are profound truths if we will take the time to consider what Jesus is saying.

Jesus begins by telling us that all authority in heaven and on Earth is his. This is important because he wants us to know that when we evangelize we are not on a rogue mission, given to us from someone without power over this world. It's a command from Jesus, who has all the authority, and therefore, our efforts will not be in vain. The creator of the Earth is telling us to evangelize the Earth.

The idea of Jesus' absolute authority is also an important reminder that Jesus has the authority, not us, so we shouldn't be so quick to redefine the methods of evangelism away from what Jesus asked us to do. The authority is his and we should honor his actual commands on making disciples, not merely the spirit of his commands.

Next, Jesus tells us who can become his disciples. He tells us that all nations are to be evangelized (as opposed to only Israel, or only the Jews). This means that wherever you live geographically, or culturally, is a place where he wants disciples. Evangelism doesn't necessarily require going on a mission trip or serving a different people group, as some people interpret this verse as saying. However, it does require that you "go," meaning you make an actual effort to leave your isolation and attempt to make disciples.

This is why so many people neglect evangelism. It's considered something that can only be done in another country when it's actually something that should be done in your own community also. It's not more spiritual to make a disciple in a foreign country. You can "go" in your own city, just as easily as you can "go" to a foreign country. Besides, the best people to evangelize a community are sometimes those that live in it. Otherwise, the language barrier, and the lack of understanding regarding cultural nuances, make it very difficult to be understood.

Jesus then tells us the procedure to follow. It's not complicated, but it is almost completely ignored. When we make someone a disciple, which is just another word for

Christian (Acts 11:26), we are to baptize them in the name of the Father, and of the Son, and of the Holy Spirit, and we are to teach them to obey everything that Jesus has commanded us. Two things, and only two things are required: baptism and teaching the red letters. Let me ask you some questions to reflect on:

- If you are a Christian, when you became a Christian did someone baptize you and teach you to obey everything that Jesus commanded (not some things, but everything)?

- If you are a Christian, when you help someone become a Christian do you baptize them and teach them to obey everything Jesus commanded (not some things, but everything)?

- If you are a Christian, the next time you help someone become a Christian are you going to baptize them and teach them to obey everything that Jesus commanded (not some things, but everything)?

- If you plan on completely ignoring Jesus' straightforward command on how to evangelize and make Christians then what gives you this right?

I know these questions are uncomfortable. These were the questions I asked myself before starting a Red Letter Church and I didn't like the answers I gave. I had faithfully baptized people, but I only taught a few of Jesus' commands to newly minted Christians. I definitely didn't teach everything he commanded, and I had all the excuses in the world:

- No one is doing it this way, so it doesn't matter if I do.

- It's going to take forever. There has to be a more efficient way to do this.

- I'm not one of the disciples he was speaking to that day, so the command isn't for me. It was a command for them.

- The whole Bible is important, so why would I focus so much on the red letters?

I'll address my weak excuses one by one.

First, it doesn't matter how many people are in disobedience as it will never change the truth of the command.

Second, Jesus isn't as concerned with efficiency as we are. It took him three years to train 12 apostles and even one of them didn't make it. After his death only 120 people were numbered among the brothers. Besides, it doesn't matter how efficient you are if the roots of new converts are so shallow that they will never make it to the end anyway.

Third, logically, if the original disciples heard this command to make disciples, then one of the commands they would teach as a part of everything is the command to make disciples. This would repeat indefinitely until I was taught to make disciples this same way. Basically, the great commission is a command itself, and so will be taught to each new generation of disciples anew. There is no way to excuse myself from the Jesus method of making disciples.

From this logic it is also true that all Christians are "Christian-making Christians." The Great Commission (as Matthew 28:18-20 is often called) is not reserved for a special priesthood, but rather the responsibility of all Christians. Everyone in a Red Letter Church has the capacity to be their own movement.

I have witnessed individuals, in my living room, multiply and become their own Church gathering through disciple making. It didn't require a complicated strategy or a budget. It was organic and natural. This is plausible when you realize that Jesus never commanded us to plant churches. He commanded us to make disciples, and from that endeavor churches emerge. In a great twist of irony, if your goal is to plant a church you may not be making disciples, but if you make disciples you always have a viable church.

Fourth, the whole Bible is important and inspired, but our current revelation from God, for our time, and for our covenant, is found in the red letters of Jesus. This is why Jesus said he is our only teacher:

Matthew 23:8-10

But you are not to be called 'Rabbi', for one is your teacher, the Christ, and all of you are brothers. Call no man on the earth your father, for one is your Father, he who is in heaven. Neither be called masters, for one is your master, the Christ.

It is not appropriate to view anyone else's words as being on the same level as Jesus' words. The above remarks were made to his apostles, the authors and sources of the New Testament, yet even their words were not to be elevated above Jesus' words, according to Jesus himself. We have one, and only one, teacher. It makes sense that to make someone a Christian we should look to the words of Christ. Paul echoes this teaching in his first letter to the Corinthians:

---

1 Corinthians 1:11-13

For it has been reported to me concerning you, my brothers, by those who are from Chloe's household, that there are contentions among you. Now I mean this, that each one of you says, "I follow Paul," "I follow Apollos," "I follow Cephas," and, "I follow Christ." Is Christ divided? Was Paul crucified for you? Or were you baptized into the name of Paul?

Paul had no interest in creating his own version of Christianity apart from the teachings of Jesus. In the same letter to the Corinthians Paul also says the following:

---

1 Corinthians 3:10-11

According to the grace of God which was given to me, as a wise master builder I laid a foundation, and another builds on it. But let each man be careful how he builds on it. For no one can lay any other foundation than that which has been laid, which is Jesus Christ.

In fact, Paul is even careful to show us that everything he says is not directly from the Lord (1 Corinthians 7:12). I wonder how many Christians would currently call themselves "Pauline Christians" if they were honest with themselves. The reason that Jesus' words can be elevated to such a privileged place, while Paul feels the need to qualify some of his words as being his own opinion, is quite simply because Jesus is God, and Jesus' words are the words of God. Jesus bluntly told us this:

> ## John 14:10
>
> *Don't you believe that I am in the Father, and the Father in me? The words that I tell you, I speak not from myself; but the Father who lives in me does his works.*

Black Letters or Black List

Some of you all reading this, especially those who have a high view of the scriptures, may be a little uneasy with my emphasis on the red letters. You might assume that this is some ploy to remove Paul or other voices from the New Testament. Rest assured, my view of the black letters (things in the Bible that were not said by Jesus) couldn't be higher. I believe the 66 books of the canon to be the inspired words of God. My church has spent stretches as long as five years just going over the letters of Paul and the other New Testament epistles, word for word and verse by verse. The reason that a Red Letter Church should see the black letters as important and inspired is because this reflects the view that Jesus himself had of scripture.

Let's first consider the Old Testament scriptures. When Jesus was tempted by Satan he quoted the Old Testament to combat Satan. He explicitly told Satan that "Man shall not live on bread alone, but by every word that proceeds out of God's mouth." (Matthew 4:4). Jesus later told the Jews that "the scriptures can't be broken." (John 10:35). In Jesus' longest recorded prayer he tells God that "your word is truth" (John 17:17). In Jesus' Sermon on the Mount he says, "Don't think that I came to destroy the law or the prophets. I didn't come to destroy, but to fulfill." (Matthew 5:17). In a discussion with the Pharisees and scribes, Jesus said, "Why do you also disobey the commandment of God because of your tradition?" (Matthew 15:3). I could list more proof texts, but these will suffice as powerful statements by Jesus about his view of the Old Testament scriptures.

Now, let's consider the New Testament. Obviously the New Testament wasn't written until after Jesus ascended back to heaven. This means that we don't have examples of him interacting with the New Testament during his life and ministry, like we do with the Old Testament. However, this doesn't mean that we are left without Jesus' guidance on the New Testament.

Jesus told Peter that, "I will give to you the keys of the Kingdom of Heaven, and whatever you bind on earth will have been bound in heaven; and whatever you release on earth will have been released in heaven." (Matthew 16:19). This seems to be a strong endorsement that the judgements and decisions of Peter would have eternal significance. Couldn't the binding and releasing happen in the form of letters that he wrote?

Jesus also told his disciples before sending them out to preach that, "Whoever will not receive you nor hear you, as you depart from there, shake off the dust that is under your feet for a testimony against them. Assuredly, I tell you, it will be more tolerable for Sodom and Gomorrah in the day of judgment than for that city!" (Mark 6:11). This isn't a blanket statement endorsing everything his apostles will ever teach or write, but it does pertain to their preaching and teaching of the kingdom that they received from Jesus (which is what we primarily find in the black letters of the New Testament). We must listen to the apostles when they teach about the kingdom.

In one of his last discussions with his apostles, Jesus said, "But the Counselor, the Holy Spirit, whom the Father will send in my name, will teach you all things, and will remind you of all that I said to you." (John 14:26). The Holy Spirit was given to the apostles to teach them all things and to help them remember everything Jesus said to them.

Jesus has a high view of the New Testament, as he does the Old Testament, even though it wasn't written during his life. Jesus endorsed the work and words of his apostles. This is why Peter even considered the letters of Paul to be scripture (2 Peter 3:16). The question isn't whether the black letters are inspired by God (they are). The question is whether we use the red letters to interpret the black letters or the black letters to interpret the red letters.

If we see the absolute authority resting in the person of Jesus, and we see the authority of the apostles as a derivative authority that he gave them, then it will change the way we interpret the New Testament. We must become intimately familiar with the red letters, and then we must interpret the rest of the New Testament in light of the clear truth that Jesus spoke.

Jesus and Paul never contradicted each other, but if you primarily use the words of Jesus to understand Paul then you'll have a much more accurate view of Christianity than if you primarily use the words of Paul to understand Jesus. Be a disciple of Jesus who also learns from Paul. Don't be a disciple of Paul who also learns from Jesus.

In practice, if we start with Romans, and then study the Sermon on the Mount and try to make it fit within Paul's theology, then we will probably end up with a different interpretation than if we start with the Sermon on the Mount and make Romans fit into Jesus' theology. Again, this isn't because Jesus and Paul are in disagreement. Rather, this is because Jesus has been ignored for so long that a unique interpretation of Paul has emerged that doesn't even try to harmonize with the words of Jesus. This is a tragedy of epic proportions.

Practical Application

Let's move on to practical matters. You are probably wondering how I have actually obeyed the command to teach everything that Jesus commanded. I have done it a few different ways. Sometimes I simply get together with the person who was recently baptized, or will be baptized soon, and we read through the red letters of the New Testament for a few hours each week until we are finished. We only read a few sentences at a time, and I make sure to "teach them to obey" not merely read the text read aloud. There is a difference.

When you teach someone to obey you must first help them understand what the words mean. If they are unfamiliar with Jesus then they will have some difficulty understanding what some of his teachings are actually trying to communicate. Then, if you are going to teach them to obey, you must help them examine their life in light of the red letters. If something needs to be repented of then the conversation should go there.

Other times, if there are a number of people who are new Christians at the same time in our group, then we use our time together on Sunday's to read through the red letters together. We still process each verse to make sure people are being taught to obey, and not just being exposed to his words. Jesus doesn't tell us the exact way that we are to teach others everything he commanded, so I feel some flexibility here. However, no matter the format you use I would encourage you to make it personal and thorough.

Whenever I teach a new Christian to obey everything that Jesus commanded I am always convicted of my own sin, and my own ignorance. I never leave a session feeling anything other than poor in spirit. This might be the brilliance behind Jesus' method. By forcing us to be the vehicle of transmission he effectively deepens our own understanding and commitment while making new disciples at the same time. I believe that Jesus is a genius, and that deviance from his commands probably has unintended consequences that we sometimes don't even grasp. Maybe tracts and sinner's prayers are short-circuiting the beautiful plan of evangelism that Jesus gave us.

It's also worth addressing the reality that some people will walk away after you have invested massive amounts of time into them. I can't keep track of the number of men and women that I have devoted months and months to, only to have them leave our group, or leave God altogether. Even as I write this all the memories flood back into my mind of the people that I couldn't help in the way I intended to. You must realize that this is a part of making disciples and it always will be a part of making disciples. This is why Jesus gave the parable of the soils.

> **Matthew 13:18-23**
>
> *"Hear, then, the parable of the farmer. When anyone hears the word of the Kingdom and doesn't understand it, the evil one comes and snatches away that which has been sown in his heart. This is what was sown by the roadside. What was sown on the rocky places, this is he who hears the word and immediately with joy receives it; yet he has no root in himself, but endures for a while. When oppression or persecution arises because of the word, immediately he stumbles. What was sown among the thorns, this is he who hears the word, but the cares of this age and the deceitfulness of riches choke the word, and he becomes unfruitful. What was sown on the good ground, this is he who hears the word and understands it, who most certainly bears fruit and produces, some one hundred times as much, some sixty, and some thirty."*

Of the four kinds of soil, only one of them was good soil that produced fruit. In my experience this is accurate. Sometimes you pour yourself into someone only for them to leave, but every once in a while you pour yourself into someone and they produce fruit forever. We must never give up, or be dejected, because of the world's inability to see the Son and his kingdom clearly. We see it, and some of those we serve will see it also. We must not dwell on our failures. Our goal is to be faithful to the command and rejoice when good soil is found.

I want to close this chapter with an analogy of why it is so important to faithfully teach the next generation of Christians to obey everything that Jesus commanded. When I was a kid we had cassette tapes for music. It was possible to make a copy of a cassette tape, but there was a problem. Every time you made a copy some of the original information was lost. At first it was almost unnoticeable. However, eventually the voices started to sound garbled and unintelligible. Ultimately, after copies had been made of copies for a few iterations, then the cassette tape was unusable. It didn't contain any of the original information from the source material that started the process.

This same problem occurs in our disciple making. Jesus is the perfect teacher. If I forget to teach the next generation of Christians a few of his commands, and they forget to teach the generation after them a few of his other commands, then eventually we are trying to make disciples with a few sentences on a tract and we don't even realize how much of the message is missing or destroyed.

You must take the burden of teaching everything Jesus commanded seriously. We wonder why our churches are anemic, filled with bickering, politically driven, and obsessed with the world's values, but it really isn't hard to understand. Most people, in most churches, have never been taught to obey everything that Jesus commanded, so why would they reflect Jesus? We wouldn't expect a group of people who have never been to medical school to be able to perform surgeries. Why would we expect a group of people who have never studied at the feet of Jesus to be able to understand his teachings and embody them in their lives?

Many things are broken because our missional methods are broken. Until we stop ignoring Jesus' teachings on making disciples we will be left with lukewarm Christians in lukewarm churches, spewing religious language with no connection to the vine. Red Letter Churches enjoy a level of depth, connection, and love that few Christians ever get to experience because we are desperately trying to be faithful copies of our Lord Jesus. A church that embraces their mission is a church that embraces each other.

CHAPTER 3 / DISCIPLESHIP

HOW DID JESUS TELL US TO LIVE?

Discipleship Is Imitation

Being baptized and being taught to obey all that Jesus commanded is not the end of the maturation process, but only the beginning. When you first study the red letters you may be filled with confidence and enthusiasm regarding your newfound knowledge, but the goal isn't knowledge, it's imitation. Discipleship is the lifelong process of becoming like Jesus, who is now your Lord and master. The longer you follow Jesus the more like him you should become and the less like him you should feel like you are. Maturity is sobering.

We've complicated discipleship to the point that we don't even know what it means to imitate Jesus in our daily life. Ask three people how Jesus would respond in a given situation and you are likely to get three different answers. We barely recall how Jesus responded to actual situations he encountered during his life, so extrapolating his behavior across time and into unique scenarios seems almost impossible.

This is where the Sermon on the Mount is paramount. Anyone who claims to be deepening their imitation of Christ while ignoring the Sermon on the Mount is misguided. The Sermon on the Mount is Jesus' Magnum Opus. It is the most radical thing that has ever been preached by a Christian, and to this day, even alluding to the idea that we take it seriously can cause people to become uncomfortable. I became a Christian in college, over twenty-two years ago, and this sermon still challenges me to my core. The Sermon on the Mount is the answer to the question of true discipleship.

In the Sermon on the Mount Jesus addresses: Hate, Lust, Adultery, Divorce, Oaths, Revenge, Giving, Prayer, Fasting, Money, Worry, Judging Others, God, Judgment, Prophets, Discipleship, and much, much, more. It touches on topics that are fundamental to the human experience, and he gives us a countercultural way to navigate every issue that he addresses. Jesus turns everything you think you know upside down, and forces you to see the world through the eyes of God. It is a distillation of Jesus' ethics and a reshaping of what it means to be a human in the image of God.

Many ethical teachers focus on actions, but the wisdom of Jesus is to focus our attention on matters of the heart, which inevitably leads to actions. Jesus goes one layer deeper than expected, and this is where the power of the sermon lives. If you shape your heart around the contours of this sermon then you will imitate Jesus instinctively without needing to have a theological debate about how Jesus would have us act.

This sermon is beyond important.

The Sermon on the Mount seems to be a sermon that Jesus gave in various cities as he traveled. We see fragments of it in different places in the Bible, but the main thrust of it is in Matthew 5-7. Before I say anything more about the Sermon on the Mount I need you to put down this book and go read this sermon for yourself. This book, of much lesser value, will be here when you return. I'll wait.

Ok, you read it? Good.

Objections To The Sermon On The Mount

Now that you've read it, do you want to know the two most common complaints against it? First, some people say that it was only written to show the severity of our sin which deepens our need for a savior, and that it was never actually intended to set a new standard of obedience. The other complaint is that it was actually an Old Testament artifact and is not even a part of the new covenant since it took place before the cross. I'm not kidding.

Let's briefly consider both of these objections. First, if Jesus meant for the Sermon on the Mount to be an impossible rubric that only deepens our need for the cross then he forgot to tell us that. It seems like quite an oversight if Jesus forgot to tell us that he didn't intend for us to actually follow his clear commands. Here is what Jesus does say at the end of the sermon:

Matthew 7:24-27

Therefore everyone who hears these words of mine and puts them into practice is like a wise man who built his house on the rock. The rain came down, the streams rose, and the winds blew and beat against that house; yet it did not fall, because it had its foundation on the rock. But everyone who hears these words of mine and does not put them into practice is like a foolish man who built his house on sand. The rain came down, the streams rose, and the winds blew and beat against that house, and it fell with a great crash.

Let me ask you a simple question. As you read the above scriptures, which is how he ended the Sermon on the Mount, do you think Jesus intended for us to obey his words? Yes or no? If Jesus actually meant for us to see our need for the cross as opposed to actually obeying his words then he is one of the worst communicators I have ever encountered.

Second, do we really believe that almost everything God said when he became a man is nullified because it doesn't fit into our small little covenantal boxes? Of course not. In fact, Jesus tells us plainly in the beginning of the sermon that his teachings are the teachings of the kingdom of heaven, not just the Old Testament.

> **Matthew 5:19**
>
> *Therefore anyone who sets aside one of the least of these commands and teaches others accordingly will be called least in the kingdom of heaven, but whoever practices and teaches these commands will be called great in the kingdom of heaven.*

It is clear that these commands are for us, those in the new covenant, in the kingdom. These are our commands. Besides, how would the Great Commission (which was spoken after the cross) make any sense if almost everything that Jesus taught us during his ministry was nullified because he said it before the cross happened? What would it mean to "teach everything he commanded" if almost everything he commanded was nullified?

The truth is that God became a man and spoke clearly and directly to us, and we marginalize it with our pseudo-intellectualism. Christians love Jesus' birth, and we love his death, but we have no idea what to do with his ethical teachings in the middle of his life. We've reduced Jesus to his bookends, and then we wonder why our faith isn't radical and why our churches are stagnate.

Memorization, Application, Transformation

So how should we use the Sermon on the Mount to deepen our imitation of Christ? The first goal is to become intimately familiar with the sermon. I used to go on a daily run years ago, and so I decided to use the time to memorize the Sermon on the Mount. I enjoy electronic music, so I took an audio file of a narrator reading the sermon and I overlaid it on top of an electronic beat, and I listened to it on a loop while I ran. A few months into the experiment the Sermon on the Mount had become a part of me. I knew it backwards and forwards.

Likewise, my wife decided that the daily Bible study that she does with our kids each day, before they start their home school, should be centered around the sermon also.

All three of my boys can quote the Sermon on the Mount naturally as it's now a part of their internal algorithm.

I would encourage you to find a way to memorize the sermon also. You've memorized countless songs, you surely have the capacity to memorize some of the most important words ever spoken. I am not saying this to weigh you down with an unbiblical burden, but just as an encouragement, as I know that memorization is a fundamental part of application.

Once you have the Sermon on the Mount memorized now you have to actually "be transformed by the renewal of your mind," as Paul wrote to the Romans. You must begin applying the wisdom of the sermon to any and every situation in which you find yourself.

- If you have children then parent them like Jesus by using the wisdom of the sermon.

- If you own a business then operate it like Jesus by using the wisdom of the sermon.

- If you work for a living then be an employee like Jesus by using the wisdom of the sermon.

- If you are a student then be a student like Jesus by using the wisdom of the sermon.

- If you are a son or daughter then be a child like Jesus by using the wisdom of the sermon.

- If you are a leader then lead like Jesus by using the wisdom of the sermon.

- If you are a follower then follow like Jesus by using the wisdom of the sermon.

- Whoever you are, be that person, but be that person like Jesus by using the wisdom of the sermon.

This may seem straightforward, but the application of the Sermon on the Mount to our actual everyday lives is not the goal of many people's discipleship. We sometimes think that discipleship and imitating Jesus is lobbying to change legislature in Washington D.C., or starting initiatives, or rallying against something on social media, or going to a foreign country on a mission trip, but these grand public overtures run the risk of missing the simple beauty of imitating Jesus in the natural course of our lives. Jesus wants us to be ordinary radicals. He's looking for ordinary people who radically imitate Him.

We need plumbers who imitate Jesus with every sink they install. We need nurses who imitate Jesus with every procedure they administer. We need truck drivers who imitate Jesus with every mile they drive. We need software engineers who imitate Jesus with every line of code they write. We need moms and dads who imitate Jesus with every diaper they change. We need you, as you, just Jesusfied. Discipleship is not about quitting your responsibilities to focus on a grander mission, but rather elevating your responsibilities to become the grand mission.

Next, after memorization, and application, comes a third phase of discipleship I call transformation. This is when you see the world for what it is, like the curtain has been pulled back and you are peering behind the stage. The best way to describe it is that you start to feel like an alien on your home planet. The familiar becomes odd. The idols you once loved become interesting artifacts of an older version of yourself. It's a rebirth in the middle of your life.

When you become transformed you live for an audience of one. You do things for your Father's eyes, not the world's eyes. Your good deeds should be numerous but not for notoriety. Your convictions should be honest before God regardless of the world's reaction. Hearing "well done good and faithful servant" at the end of your life becomes more important than a million followers or a million dollars.

It is your responsibility to live a life of discipleship in imitation of Christ. Others can help, but you must "work out your own salvation with trembling and fear" (Philippians 2:12). How are you going to move through the phases of memorization, application, and transformation?

You may have noticed that there is an incredible similarity between mission and discipleship. They are essentially the same thing, but serve different purposes. Mission is when you teach someone about Jesus for the first time. Discipleship is learning at the feet of Jesus for the rest of your life. Mission is you to the world. Discipleship is Jesus to you.

Despite their similarities, it's important that we uphold mission and discipleship as two separate functions in the church. Without mission the church doesn't grow. Without discipleship the individuals don't grow. A church on mission that lacks discipleship will never stand the test of time. Growing in numbers without growing in the imitation of Christ is a recipe for an angry church split, not organic Godly growth. The alternative is also lacking. Personal depth with Jesus without mission causes the church to become a holy huddle. This is when the church begins caring more about their own comfort and predictable rhythms than new people being saved. A healthy church must have both mission and discipleship.

Another unforeseen consequence of elevating mission while neglecting discipleship (which is not uncommon), is that the further you drift from Jesus the worse disciples you will make. Jesus rebuked the Pharisees for this very problem.

Matthew 23:15

Woe to you, scribes and Pharisees, hypocrites, because you travel around on sea and land to make one proselyte; and when he becomes one, you make him twice as much a son of hell as yourselves.

Mission is not praiseworthy in and of itself. Spreading misinformation is not admirable, even if we paint it in religious language like the Pharisees. For a mission to be meaningful it must be coupled with discipleship. Our discipleship is the difference between making disciples of Jesus or making sons of hell.

CHAPTER 4 / COMMUNITY

HOW DID JESUS TELL US TO GATHER?

The Sunday Circus

When you walk into a church service on a Sunday morning you are likely to see some of the following, depending on your denomination:

- There will be a preacher on a stage who speaks for the majority of the service, while the congregation sits quietly with their backs to each other. Jesus never depicted the church gathering this way.

- The service will take place in a large building that can facilitate hundreds or thousands of people. Jesus never depicted the church gathering this way.

- Communion will be taken quarterly or almost never, and it will consist of a cracker and a shot of grape juice. Jesus never depicted the church gathering this way.

- There will be soundboards, sound engineers, and a professional band who plays whenever the preacher isn't talking. Jesus never depicted the church gathering this way.

- There might even be a fancy robe worn by the preacher. Jesus never depicted the church gathering this way.

Is anything I listed above a sin? It's not a sin to preach a sermon. It's not a sin to rent out a building to do it in. It's not a sin to eat crackers and grape juice. It's not a sin to listen to a band. It's not a sin to wear funny robes. So...no, none of those things are sinful. However, if those ingredients don't equal up to church, as commanded by Jesus, then you will need to separately find a time to gather as a church, even if you have a weekly habit of listening to a sermon from a robed man, interspersed with a band, while munching on crackers and grape juice. These things may not be a sin, but they definitely aren't church either.

The First Church Gathering

For most Christians, the idea that Jesus told us how to do our church gatherings is a new concept. They either believe that tradition is the master of Sunday services, or they believe that we can do virtually anything we want during our gatherings as long as it sounds religious enough. The question is: what if there is a Jesus centered approach to our Sunday church gatherings that originated as a direct command from Jesus himself? For all the reasons mentioned in the chapters on the gospel, mission, and discipleship, if Jesus gave us clear directions on our church gatherings then we should obey him completely.

To start this journey, let's look at the Last Supper. This may be surprising, but the Last Supper was actually the first church service ever recorded. As you'll notice in the passage on the next page, Jesus is not just eating with his disciples for nourishment. He is also setting the standard for what our time together as Christians should look like. As you'll see, he gives us a direct command to "do this in remembrance of him."

> ### Luke 14-20
>
> *When the hour had come, he sat down with the twelve apostles.* He said to them, *"I have earnestly desired to eat this Passover with you before I suffer, for I tell you, I will no longer by any means eat of it until it is fulfilled in God's Kingdom."* He received a cup, and when he had given thanks, he said, *"Take this, and share it among yourselves, for I tell you, I will not drink at all again from the fruit of the vine, until God's Kingdom comes."*
>
> *He took bread, and when he had given thanks, he broke, and gave it to them, saying,* "This is my body which is given for you. Do this in memory of me." *Likewise, he took the cup after supper, saying,* "This cup is the new covenant in my blood, which is poured out for you."

The Passover was a meal that the Jews ate to remember the day that God "passed over" their homes, sparing them from the judgment of the Egyptians. God "passed over" the homes with the literal blood of a lamb on their door frames. The Jews with the lamb's blood were spared from death visiting their homes.

Jesus reinterprets this meal to be about himself. It is no longer about the lamb's body and the lamb's blood, but rather, it is now a celebration of Jesus' body and Jesus' blood. Jesus is the true lamb, slain to save us from death. Jesus reimagines a symbol of the old covenant to be a symbol of the new covenant. The bread is Jesus' body and the wine is Jesus' blood. The last Passover became the first Lord's Supper.

Jesus then explicitly tells us to, "do this in memory of me." Here is the incredible part of that command: the apostles interpreted this as the reason we get together on Sunday and the primary thing we do when we get together on Sunday.

For instance, the Corinthian church had forgotten what the Lord's Supper was all about, and Paul had to remind them of Jesus' teachings on this topic. He spent quite a bit of time in his letter to the Corinthians addressing how the church should take the Lord's Supper.

This is important because it allows us to see how an apostle like Paul continued in the teachings of Jesus, and it also shows us exactly what Paul taught his churches to do on Sundays when they get together. As you read the following passage just consider how different their church gathering looked compared to our typical Sunday event.

1 Corinthians 11:20-27

When therefore you assemble yourselves together, it is not the Lord's supper that you eat. For in your eating each one takes his own supper first. One is hungry, and another is drunken. What, don't you have houses to eat and to drink in? Or do you despise God's assembly and put them to shame who don't have enough? What shall I tell you? Shall I praise you? In this I don't praise you.

For I received from the Lord that which also I delivered to you, that the Lord Jesus on the night in which he was betrayed took bread. When he had given thanks, he broke it and said, "Take, eat. This is my body, which is broken for you. Do this in memory of me." In the same way he also took the cup, after supper, saying, "This cup is the new covenant in my blood. Do this, as often as you drink, in memory of me." For as often as you eat this bread and drink this cup, you proclaim the Lord's death until he comes. Therefore whoever eats this bread or drinks the Lord's cup in a way unworthy of the Lord will be guilty of the body and the blood of the Lord.

Paul begins by rebuking the Corinthians because when they "assemble" they are making a mockery of the Lord's Supper. This illustrates that when they assembled the Lord's Supper was a core part of why. While some Christians are "hungry" others are consuming so much that they are "drunk." This shows us that Paul really is referring to a full meal, like the Passover would have been, because it would be very difficult to get drunk or go hungry if the expectation was to have a thimble of wine and a small cracker to partake in. The New Testament church assembled to eat a meal, a meal reinterpreted around Jesus's death for us.

Then, to make the source of this command very clear, Paul then quotes Jesus from the night when he commanded us to do this in remembrance of himself. Paul draws a direct line from the church gathering in Corinth to the first time Jesus instituted the Lord's Supper. Paul expected Christians to come together as a church and have a meal in remembrance of, and obedience to, Jesus.

The original Sunday meeting, in the scriptures, was not a canvas for our creativity, but rather a recreation of the Last Supper in remembrance of Jesus. There would have been a meal, bread to specifically represent his body, wine to specifically represent his blood, and an awareness of Jesus' absence at the table because he died for us and won't eat this meal again with us until we are reunited with him in the kingdom.

Distorting The Basics

We have distorted our community in the same way that we have distorted the gospel, mission and discipleship. We distort the gospel by ignoring Jesus' call to preach about the kingdom. We distort our mission by ignoring The Great Commission. We distort our discipleship by ignoring the Sermon on the Mount. We distort our community by ignoring The Last Supper.

Not unlike the gospel, mission, and discipleship, ignoring the true command behind our Sunday gatherings has immense unintended consequences. When the centerpiece of our time together is a meal of remembrance, instead of a concert of emotion, then we avoid the following pitfalls:

- We don't need expensive buildings because the most natural place to have an intimate meal is in a home. This is why the early church gathered in homes throughout a city (Romans 16:5, 1 Corinthians 16:19, Colossians 4:15).

- We don't need a preacher giving a monologue to entertain the crowd. In homes the church gathering consists of brothers and sisters having a dialogue, taking turns encouraging one another in the ways that they are capable of (1 Corinthians 14:26).

- We don't need a talented band. The people in the gathering can easily read Psalms, or sing a simple song, or just pray together (Ephesians 5:19, Colossians 3:16). Instruments aren't bad, but they are far from necessary either.

You will also find that true connections, and lifelong friends, emerge from eating a meal together every week. Eating a meal in the first century, or the twenty-first century, is a hallmark of our deepest friendships. Ideas are shared around meals, fears are shared around meals, and encouragement is given around meals. The early church ate together, knew each other, loved each other, and would sacrifice anything for each other, while our modern church is often an assembly of strangers.

We each desire to know others, and to be known by others, but true connection has never been more difficult. Social media has promised us friendships, but it has only fostered acquaintances. The church that Jesus started, that we get to be a part of, is still the world's best chance at being a part of an authentic community.

Listen to a depiction of the early church as recorded in Acts:

> *Acts 4:32-37*
>
> *The multitude of those who believed were of one heart and soul. Not one of them claimed that anything of the things which he possessed was his own, but they had all things in common. With great power, the apostles gave their testimony of the resurrection of the Lord Jesus. Great grace was on them all. For neither was there among them any who lacked, for as many as were owners of lands or houses sold them, and brought the proceeds of the things that were sold, and laid them at the apostles' feet, and distribution was made to each, according as anyone had need. Joses, who by the apostles was also called Barnabas (which is, being interpreted, Son of Encouragement), a Levite, a man of Cyprus by race, having a field, sold it and brought the money and laid it at the apostles' feet.*

The early church was a true community, sacrificially giving to anyone in need. It's difficult to give yourself fully to people that you don't even know. If you spend every Sunday looking at the back of someone's head then your knowledge of their true needs, and your willingness to supply for those needs, are radically diminished. When you combine a Jesus centered gospel, a Jesus centered mission, a Jesus centered discipleship, and a Jesus centered gathering, then you are unlocking the potential for radical Christ like love to take place in the church. Some of the members of our church have been the recipients of substantial gifts because our community was a true community. No one should lack anything.

This may be surprising, but many of the scriptures that are used by some preachers on Sunday mornings in order to get us to give to the church (primarily for the sake of salaries and leases), are actually verses about the church giving to other needy people in the church (2 Corinthians 9:6-8 is a great example of a verse about giving to the poor that is often used to support giving to the church for buildings and salaries). Once we start ignoring the commands of Jesus about Sunday gatherings then we find ourselves having to skew other scriptures to support our invented infrastructure. A worker is worth his wages, but this is far from a defense of corporatized church services that require immense capital to operate.

A Christianity That Can Spread Organically

Another disastrous consequence of constructing our gatherings like a concert is that concerts aren't easy to replicate. A church should be able to be started whenever a couple of disciples are together. Here is how Jesus said it:

> ### Matthew 18:20
>
> *For where two or three are gathered together in my name, there I am in the middle of them.*

In the era we find ourselves in, a church plant requires millions of dollars, complicated strategies, graphic designers, a study of demographics, musicians, and gifted orators, amongst dozens of other things that don't naturally replicate.

It's time to return to a simple version of church that emerges when two or three are gathered in the name of Jesus. If we come together in his name, no matter how small our group is, he is with us. Let's be honest, the alternative to a simple church is not exactly working anyway.

Church attendance in America is on a steep decline. What we are currently doing is not in line with Jesus' teaching, and it also isn't working to grow the faith. Consider the decline in American church attendance since 2007. "Monthly attendance or more" is down and "attendance a few times a year or less" is up.

The church as we know it is going away in America. It is imperative that we return to Jesus, and to his commands, if we want the church to thrive. Our current systems and structures are found wanting. The world does not want to be entertained by Christians—we might be the

In U.S., church attendance is declining

% of U.S. adults who say they attend religious services ...

━━ NET Monthly or more

━━ NET A few times a year or less

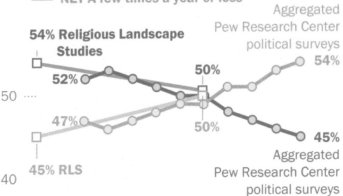

54% Religious Landscape Studies

Aggregated Pew Research Center political surveys

52%

50%

54%

47%

50%

45%

45% RLS

Aggregated Pew Research Center political surveys

50

40

30

20

10

0

2007   2009   2014   2018/'19

Source: Pew Research Center Religious Landscape Studies (2007 and 2014). Aggregated Pew Research Center political surveys conducted 2009-July 2019 on the telephone.
"In U.S., Decline of Christianity Continues at Rapid Pace"

PEW RESEARCH CENTER

worst entertainers in history. Let Hollywood entertain the world. People come to church for truth and community, two things Hollywood will always fail at. Are you going to watch the church in America die as we entertain ourselves to death, or are you going to start or join a simple church community, with a deep love for Jesus and others, that can spontaneously replicate across the world?

A Typical Sunday

So what does a typical Sunday gathering look like for our church? Here is a simple breakdown of what we do:

- People start arriving at our house around 3:30pm.

- There are about 10-20 people in total, and when it gets larger another group starts in a different house.

- We hang out for thirty minutes to an hour, usually catching up on life. We learn about the highs and lows of people's last week in casual conversations.

- The food is usually put in the oven to warm up during this time. We rotate who is responsible for food, or we do potlucks.

- We get together in a circle in the living room around 4 or 4:30pm.

- If the kids are old enough then they join us. This is usually when they are about 6 or 7 years old. If we have babies then they just stay with the moms and dads during our discussion and people will take turns going for walks with them if they cry a lot. If we have toddlers then an older kid or parent might keep an eye on them in a separate room, or they stay with us and play on the floor if it isn't too disruptive.

- We start with prayer and singing. Different people pray and lead songs. Sometimes we just pray. Sometimes we sing a single song, sometimes we sing multiple songs. We might read some Psalms.

- We then have a conversation around Scripture. We are currently reading through the gospel of John, so one of us will read a few verses then we have an open discussion about what it means, how to apply it, and other verses that it reminds us of.

- After about an hour of being in a circle, when it's about 5 or 5:30pm we take communion. It starts with a piece of bread that we all pass around, each taking a piece of it, then we pass a cup of grape juice around and dip the bread in it. Usually someone shares a thought about remembering Jesus. We pray together then we all eat the bread that was dipped in grape juice together.

- Next we take part in the rest of communion, the full meal. We get all the kids a plate first, then the adults get a plate. We sit around the house eating together and hanging out for another hour or two.

- Sometimes the dads shoot basketball in the driveway with the kids. Sometimes the mom's sit around the kitchen table and catch up more. Sometimes we put on Minecraft and try to build cool stuff. Sometimes we watch some sort of sports on TV.

- Eventually the young kids start to get fussy and it's a natural alarm for the families to start packing up.

- Everyone helps clean the house, which has become a mess by this point. We give hugs to each other, and everyone goes home.

What we do each Sunday is simple and profound. We cry together. We celebrate together. We follow Christ together. I am not asking you to consider a theory that I have about church. I am asking you to consider an ancient way of doing church, which originated with Jesus, that I have been a part of for almost 15 years. I literally cannot imagine doing church substantially differently.

You might wonder what you should do if you find yourself in a church that doesn't model their gathering off of the Last Supper. You can continue going to your existing church, but you must also create a time to get together with like minded friends to do church the way you read about in this chapter. Just start doing what you know is right and everything will become clear.

If you don't currently have ties to a church then start a Red Letter Church next Sunday. Find one person to give this book to that you think would do it with you. Don't overthink obedience.

Our church began when me and my wife decided that we were going to get together each Sunday and have a Jesus centered gathering with communion. The first week we were alone. We decided that even if we were alone for the rest of our lives that we are going to obey Jesus. That was the last Sunday we were alone. There have been people doing church with us ever since then.

We have preached the kingdom of Jesus, baptized people in backyard pools or the ocean, taught them to obey everything Jesus commanded, strived to embody the Sermon on the Mount, and gathered each Sunday to take communion and remember Jesus.

Our church has now multiplied beyond our city, and I don't think the gates of hades can overcome it (Matthew

16:18). Our Red Letter Church will last forever. It may be the smallest of all seeds, but it will become the largest of all plants (Mark 4:30-32).

We have grown at a slow rate, but we are building disciples for life. We have even had to put people out of the church on rare occasions based on Jesus' command in Matthew 18:15-20, but we continue to expand. Jesus holds us together—not our talents on a stage, not our intelligence, and not our money.

Our community is alive and well.